WHIZZY SCIENCE

Make it Glow!

Written by:
Anna Claybourne

Illustrated by:
Kimberley Scott and Venetia Dean

First published in 2013 by Wayland
Copyright © Wayland 2013

Wayland
338 Euston Road
London NW1 3BH

Wayland Australia
Hachette Children's Books
Level 17/207
Kent Street
Sydney, NSW 2000

Senior Editor: Julia Adams
Editor: Annabel Stones
Designer: Anthony Hannant (LittleRedAnt)
Illustrator (step-by-steps): Kimberley Scott
Illustrator (incidentals and final crafts): Venetia Dean
Proofreader & Indexer: Sara Harper

Dewey categorisation: 535

ISBN 978 0 7502 7733 4

Printed in China

Wayland is a division of Hachette Children's Books,
an Hachette UK company.

www.hachette.co.uk

Picture acknowledgements:
All photographs: Shutterstock;
except: p. 25: Sam Ogden/Science Photo Library.

Contents

Glow!

What makes things glow with light? Light is a kind of energy. It travels through the air, spreading out from lamps, streetlights and car headlights. Light also reaches us from much further away – from the Sun and the stars, which shine onto us here on Earth.

WOOOOAH

CLICK

LOTS OF LIGHT

There's light all around us, day and night. Long ago, people only had natural light sources, such as the Sun, Moon, stars, lightning and fires. Today, we can also light up our houses at night using electric lights. Some animals glow with their own light, like fireflies and lanternsharks. Besides light sources, light bounces off other objects to our eyes, which is how we see them.

LIFE WITHOUT LIGHT

What would life be like without the glow of light? Most people are used to depending on light to find their way, read, use a computer, or see each other. If you are completely blind, you can still use your other senses to find out about things. Light is also important for making plants grow.

LOOKING AT LIGHT

We see light because our eyes can detect it. When light enters your eyeballs, they send signals to your brain, so you can understand what you see. You don't think about it much, but your brain is constantly busy, working out what the patterns of light mean.

BEING A SCIENTIST

Use the exciting experiments in this book to try out different ways of making and using glowing light. To do experiments like a real scientist, remember:

• Follow the instructions and watch what happens carefully.

• You can record your results by writing down, sketching or taking photos of what happens.

• Real scientists do experiments a few times over to check they always work.

Light and Shadows

Experiment with making shadows to see how light works.

Here's What to Do...

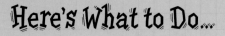

YOU WILL NEED
1) A hand-held electric torch
2) A pair of hands
3) A selection of objects of different shapes
4) A plain, flat wall

1. Use the torch to shine light at a plain, pale-coloured wall.

2. Try holding an object or your hand up to make a shadow. Twist and turn it to make different shapes.

?

3. Move your hand or object closer to the light, then further away – what happens?

?

4. Shine your torch through a see-through object, like an ice cube or clear plastic ruler. Does it have a shadow?

6

WHAT'S GOING ON?

As light shines out from a light source, it travels in straight lines, called beams or rays. If there is something in the way, the light cannot bend around it. Instead, some of the light is blocked, leaving a shadow where the light can't reach. The shadow is the same shape as the object that's in the way.

See-through or transparent objects can have shadows too. This may be because they block a little bit of the light, or because they make the light rays break up and change direction.

! TROUBLESHOOTER

Make sure you don't have other lights on in the room.

SHADOW SHAPES

You can use your hands to make shadow shapes that look like animals. Here are some to try:

WHAT NEXT?

Do coloured lights make coloured shadows? To make a coloured light, try putting coloured 3D glasses or sweet wrappers over the end of the torch.

Can you make two shadows at the same time, using two torches?

Periscope

Light goes in straight lines, but it can change direction if it bounces off a shiny surface, like a mirror.

YOU WILL NEED

1) A long, narrow cardboard box
2) Scissors
3) Modelling clay
4) Two small mirrors

Here's What to Do...

1. Cut flaps in both ends of your box, as shown.

2. Push the flaps into the box to make sloping surfaces each at a 45° angle. Hold the flaps in place by putting lumps of modelling clay behind them.

3. Stick the small mirrors onto the flaps using modelling clay.

4. Hold the box upright and look into the bottom mirror. You should be able to see what you would see if you were looking out of the top hole.

45°

45°

WHAT'S GOING ON?

When a beam of light hits a mirror, it reflects, or bounces off it. If it hits the mirror at a right angle, or 90°, it reflects straight back. If it hits at another angle, it reflects off in a different direction. The tilted mirrors in the periscope make the light beams turn round a corner, travel down inside the box, then bend out again to meet your eyes.

! TROUBLESHOOTER

If it's not working, change the angles of the mirrors by squeezing the modelling clay.

Mirror

Light

UNDERWATER VIEW

Submarines have periscopes so that the people inside can look out above the surface of the water.

Mirror

WHAT NEXT?

Try using your periscope to look over a wall or round a corner while you hide behind it.

Can you make light go on an even more complicated journey using more mirrors?

You can decorate your periscope with leaves to camouflage it.

Tea light lanterns

How can you make a tea light candle into a better, brighter light?

YOU WILL NEED
1) 4 tea light candles
2) 4 clear jam jars
3) Thin card
4) Scissors
5) A thick black felt-tip pen
6) Kitchen foil
7) Sticky tape
8) An adult to help – be careful with candles!

Here's What to Do...

1. Cut three rectangles of card. Each one should be as high as your jars and long enough to wrap halfway around them.

2. Decorate the rectangles as follows:
- Colour one in all over with the black pen.
- Cover one with a smooth layer of foil and tape it on at the back.
- Cover one with foil that has been crumpled up, then opened out again.

3. Now bend the cards around the back of three of the jars, with the decorated surface facing inwards. Tape them in place.

4. Stand the jars in a row on a safe, firm surface, along with the fourth jar with nothing behind it. Put the tea lights in and ask an adult to light them. Stand back, and look at the jars from the front. Which gives the brightest light?

WHAT'S GOING ON?

When a candle glows with light, it shines in all directions. If there is a mirror or shiny surface behind it, the light will bounce back, and more of it will shine at you. The crumpled foil makes light shoot off in all directions, so it doesn't work quite as well. The black surface doesn't reflect much light at all.

! TROUBLESHOOTER

It will be easier to see the results if you switch off any other lights in the room.

SHINY LAMPS

Car headlights and torch bulbs have curved mirrors behind them, to help as much light as possible shine forwards.

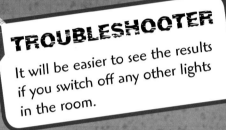

WHAT NEXT?

What happens if you try other effects, such as covering the card with glitter?

Make an indoor rainbow

This experiment shows how real rainbows are made from light.

Here's What to Do...

YOU WILL NEED
1) A clear glass
2) Water
3) A small mirror that you can get wet
4) A torch
5) White paper or card

1. Fill the glass with water.

2. Stand the mirror in the water, leaning against the side of the glass.

3. Turn the lights off and shine the torch through the water at the mirror.

4. Hold a piece of white paper or card to catch the reflected light. You should see a rainbow pattern!

WHAT'S GOING ON?

This experiment works because of something called refraction – a name for light bending. White light is made of a mixture of all the rainbow colours. When a beam of light moves from one see-through substance into another, it bends slightly. The bending makes the light split into its different colours.

! TROUBLESHOOTER

If you don't want to put your mirror in water, you can try holding it behind the glass, and shine the torch at it through the water.

In this experiment, the light shines from air into glass, then into water, then back again. So it bends and splits quite a lot – enough for you to see the colours of the rainbow.

REAL RAINBOWS

A real rainbow in the sky works the same way, but with sunlight and raindrops. Beams of sunlight shine into the raindrops, bounce off the inside and shine back out again, split into rainbow colours.

WHAT NEXT?

Try shining a torch through other clear objects, such as a clear plastic ruler, spectacle lenses, glass ornaments or crystals, to see if they make a rainbow.

Glowing envelopes, plasters and SWEETS

Explore a very unusual way of making light with these quick experiments.

YOU WILL NEED
1) Sticking plasters
2) Sugar lumps or large-grained sugar
3) A plate
4) A rolling pin
5) Self-seal envelopes
6) Crunchy sweets
7) A mirror

You need somewhere really dark for this, like a room at night, or a dark walk-in cupboard. Take care not to bump into things!

Here's What to Do...

1. Take ordinary sticking plasters – several brands if possible – and try ripping the backing off them as fast as you can.

2. Put sugar lumps or grains on a plate and crush them with a rolling pin.

3. Seal up a self-seal envelope, then rip it open again as fast as possible.

4. Take a hard but breakable sweet, like a hard, crunchy mint, and snap it in two. Or try crunching it with your mouth open in front of a mirror.

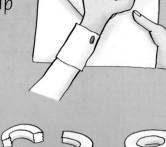

WHAT'S GOING ON?

Amazingly, doing any of these things can create sparks and flashes of bright blueish light, called triboluminescence. It happens because some chemicals spark when their atoms and molecules, the tiny parts they are made of, are pulled apart. Scientists are not sure why!

!

TROUBLESHOOTER

If you can't see anything, wait a few minutes for your eyes to adjust to the dark.

Long ago, sugar didn't come in grains or lumps. Instead, it was sold in a big, hard cone shape or 'sugar loaf'. People used to notice it sparkling and glowing when they chipped bits off in the dark.

WHAT NEXT?

Can you catch the sparks on camera or video?

Glow-in-the-dark Shapes

Experiment with glow-in-the-dark shapes or stickers, which are easy to find in toy shops.

Here's What to Do...

YOU WILL NEED

1) A packet of glow-in-the-dark stars, moons or other stickers or shapes

2) A bright torch

3) A dark room

4) A book

1. In a dark room, take the stars out of the packet and check they are not yet glowing.

2. Shine a torch on a star for a minute, then switch it off. Does the star glow? How long does it glow for before you can no longer see it?

3. Try leaving a shape for a day, in sunlight or electric light, half-covered with a book. Does it glow in the dark afterwards?

WHAT'S GOING ON?

Glow-in-the-dark shapes are made of special chemicals that store up energy when light shines on them. Then, they slowly release the energy, making them glow with light. This is called phosphorescence – you say it 'foss-for-RESS-ence'. Only the parts that get 'charged up' with light will glow later.

! TROUBLESHOOTER

You need to use shapes that aren't already glowing – if they are, keep them somewhere dark for a few hours first.

GLOWING LIFE

The word 'phosphorescent' is also sometimes used to describe living things that glow in the dark, like some mushrooms, jellyfish and plankton – though they don't work the same way.

WHAT NEXT?

How could you use glow-in-the-dark stars to leave someone a secret message? You would need to make part of each star light up to show a letter or symbol.

Make a glowing jar lantern

You can also buy glow-in-the-dark paint, which lets you make your own glowing creations!

YOU WILL NEED

1) Glow-in-the-dark paint, available from toy or craft shops
2) An empty, clear glass food jar
3) An old newspaper
4) A fine paintbrush

Here's What to Do...

1. Make sure your jar is clean and completely dry. Stand it on an old newspaper.

2. Squeeze a blob of glow-in-the-dark paint onto the newspaper.

3. Use the paintbrush to paint different sizes of dots all over the inside of the jar.

You can buy glow-in-the-dark paint in different colours, to make multicoloured lanterns.

4. Let the paint dry and stand the jar in daylight for a day so the paint can store up light energy. Then you can use it as a decoration or night light when it's dark.

WHAT'S GOING ON?

Inventors have worked out how to make glow-in-the-dark chemicals into safe, non-toxic paint for craft projects. Once it dries, it works just like a glow-in-the-dark shape or sticker.

! TROUBLESHOOTER

Work from the bottom of the jar upwards, so you don't smudge the dots you've already done.

USEFUL GLOW

As well as being fun, glow-in-the-dark paint is used on things like clocks, dials and safety signs so that people can see them in the dark.

WHAT NEXT?

People often make lots of these jars to hang up as garden lights, or to use as decorations for parties or weddings.

Glow stick photos

Glow sticks are little sticks that glow when you snap and bend them. You can use them to make a shape picture in the dark. You'll need an assistant to take the photo.

YOU WILL NEED

1) One or more glow sticks
2) A camera or cameraphone
3) A dark room

Here's What to Do...

1. Set up the camera ready to take a picture in low light, with no flash, and a long shutter speed. Ask an adult to help you set a long shutter speed of 20-30 seconds. You may be able to do this with a smartphone app, too.

2. Go into a dark room with the camera, glow stick and photographer!

3. Stand in front of the camera and break your glow stick to make it light up.

4. Wave the glow stick around quickly in a simple shape or pattern. It could be an initial, a love heart, a circle, a wiggly snake or just a squiggle. The other person should take a photo while the stick is moving.

WHAT'S GOING ON?

As long as the camera is on a low light setting with no flash it should be able to capture the fast-moving glow stick as a line or pattern on the photo. When a camera takes a picture slowly like this, there is time for light to move and change in the same photo.

! TROUBLESHOOTER

The camera should be held as still as possible. Rest it on a piece of furniture, or use a tripod if you have one.

WHAT NEXT?

Try looking at a glow stick or lamp in the dark for a few seconds, then shut your eyes. You should still be able to see the shape of the stick! When bright light hits the light-sensing retina at the back of your eye, it makes it less sensitive. Afterwards, you can still see the shape where the retina is not working as well.

21

Glowing water stream

This experiment lets you make light curve along a stream of water. It works best in a fairly dark room. (Don't switch the lights off until the experiment is set up!)

YOU WILL NEED

1) A clear plastic drinks bottle
2) A nail
3) Water
4) A torch
5) A large plastic bowl
6) A table and chair
7) An adult to help

Here's What to Do...

1. Ask an adult to make a hole in the side of the bottle, near the bottom, with the nail.

2. Put the plastic bowl on a chair next to the table.

3. Cover the hole and fill the bottle with water. Put it on the table with the hole towards the bowl.

4. Shine the torch through the other side of the bottle, through the water and at the hole.

5. Uncover the hole so that water flows out and into the bowl, taking the light with it.

WHAT'S GOING ON?

As the light beam moves along inside the water, it actually reflects off the inside surface of the water stream. It bounces to and fro, meaning it can travel wherever the water stream takes it.

! **TROUBLESHOOTER**

It could be messy! Put an old towel or newspaper on the floor to catch drips.

OPTICAL FIBRES

Your water stream is just like a real optical fibre, a bendy tube made of glass for carrying light. Optical fibres can be used to make lamps, or to light up the insides of people's bodies so doctors can look for problems. We also use them to carry computer signals, in the form of on-and-off patterns of light.

WHAT NEXT?

If you have a laser pointer, try using that instead of a torch – it may work even better.

Laser jelly

Jelly experiments are a great way to find out how light can bounce, bend and travel in different directions. For this you need a laser pointer.

YOU WILL NEED
1) A packet of red or yellow jelly
2) A shallow tray or baking tray
3) Cooking oil
4) A non-sharp knife and pastry cutters
5) A laser pointer

Be careful with laser pointers and don't shine them at your eyes.

Here's What to Do...

1. Make up the jelly using a little less water than usual. Grease the tray with a little oil and pour in the jelly to set.

2. When it's set, cut the jelly into shapes such as strips, D-shapes, squares, triangles and circles, using smooth pastry cutters or a knife.

3. Carefully lift out the shapes and lie them on a flat table top.

4. Now try shining your laser pointer into the jelly shapes from the side. What happens if you...

• Shine it into the flat side of a D-shape?

• Shine it along inside a jelly strip and wave it from side to side?

• Shine it through a square or triangle?

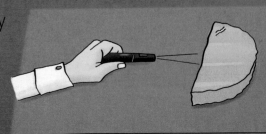

WHAT'S GOING ON?

Depending on the shapes you use, and the angles you point at, different things will happen to your beam of laser light. It may reflect off the inside of a jelly shape, and bounce back out. Or it may shine through a shape, but bend because of refraction.

! **TROUBLESHOOTER**

Make it a bit darker in the room if it's hard to see what's happening.

WHAT'S GOING ON?

WHAT NEXT?

Try other colours of jelly. Do they work as well?

Can you make a flexible jelly strip into an optical fibre by bending it?

Camera obscura

The first ever type of camera, invented around 1000 years ago, captures a moving picture made of light! You need a room that you can make very dark even when it's bright and sunny outside.

YOU WILL NEED

1) A room with a small window facing a plain, white or light coloured wall
2) A large piece of cardboard or thick black cloth
3) Strong masking or packing tape
4) Pointy scissors or a sharp pencil

Here's What to Do...

1. Cover the window completely with the cloth or cardboard and fix it with masking tape around the sides so no light can get in.

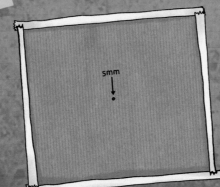

5mm

2. Ask an adult to make a small, neat hole in the middle of the card or cloth with the pencil or scissors. About 5 mm across works best.

3. Turn off the light in the room (take care). You should now be able to see a detailed image of what's outside on the wall opposite the window.

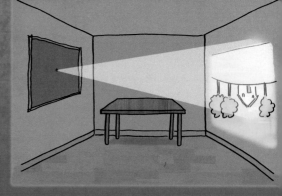

4. Look out for people, trees, clouds or cars moving! What do you notice about the image?

26

WHAT'S GOING ON?

This type of camera is called a camera obscura, which simply means 'dark room'. The small hole lets in beams of light from the objects outside. As they travel in straight lines, beams from high up end up low down on the wall, and vice versa, so the image is upside down.

TROUBLESHOOTER

Once the room is dark, it will be easy to spot any gaps around your blind and seal them up with tape.

LIGHT SCIENTIST

A scientist known as Alhazen, living in Egypt around the year 1020, studied the camera obscura and figured out how it worked. He also realised that our eyeballs work in the same way.

Big camera obscuras like this one in Edinburgh, UK, capture images of the whole city around them.

WHAT NEXT?

Can you make a smaller camera obscura inside a box?

Ultraviolet glow

An ultraviolet (UV) lamp or 'blacklight' shines ultraviolet light. This is a type of high-energy light that is invisible to humans. However, it makes some substances, such as tonic water, glow with light that you can see.

YOU WILL NEED
1) A blacklight or UV torch
2) A bottle of tonic water
3) Laundry liquid
4) Bright white paper
5) Whitening toothpaste
6) Petroleum jelly
7) Overripe bananas

Here's What to Do...

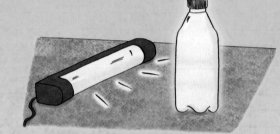

1. Shine your blacklight at the bottle of tonic water in the dark. You will see it glowing bright blue all the way through.

2. Test other substances to see if they glow in a blacklight. You may have some luck with bright white paper, laundry liquid (don't let it touch your skin), whitening toothpaste, petroleum jelly, or even the black spots on ripe bananas.

3. Make secret messages that can only be seen using a blacklight, by writing with a brush and laundry liquid, then leaving it to dry.

TOP SECRET SCIENCE EXPERIMENT

WHAT'S GOING ON?

Some substances naturally glow in UV light, such as quinine, found in tonic water. Normal sunlight contains some UV light. So by adding these substances to things like laundry liquid and toothpaste, we can make things like teeth and white clothes appear extra bright and glowing.

You can find small UV torches and lamps at hardware shops. An adult should help you with this.

Scorpions also glow in UV light!

TONIC

WHAT NEXT?

Freeze tonic water inside a clean rubber glove to make an ice hand that you can stand in a bowl of punch for a spooky party. Use your blacklight to light it up!

29

Glossary

atoms Tiny units that substances are made of.

beam A line of light travelling forwards through space.

blacklight A light or lamp that gives out ultraviolet light.

camera obscura A dark room or box with a hole that lets in light beams to form an image inside.

energy The power to do work or make things happen.

light source Something that light shines out of.

molecules Groups of atoms that make up substances.

optical fibre A bendy tube made of glass.

plankton Tiny plants and animals found in seawater.

phosphorescent Able to soak up light energy, then glow for some time.

ray A line of light travelling forwards through space.

reflect To bounce off a surface.

refraction The way light bends when it moves from one clear substance into another.

transparent See-through, or able to let light through.

triboluminescence Sparks of light given off by some substances when they break or tear.

ultraviolet (UV) light A type of high-energy light that humans can't see.

further reading

BOOKS:

Experiments with Light and Colour
by Tom Jackson, Gareth Stevens
Publishing, 2010

Bright Ideas: The Science of Light
by Jay Hawkins, Windmill Books, 2013

Tales of Invention: The Light Bulb
by Chris Oxlade, Raintree, 2011

WEBSITES

Science Kids: Light
www.sciencekids.co.nz/light.html

Optics for Kids
www.optics4kids.org/

Index

Whizzy SCIENCE
Titles in the series:

Make it Zoom!
978 0 7502 7732 7

Zooming cars
Straw shooter
Heli-zoomer
Zero-gravity water squirt
Zooming balloon rocket
Magazine tug-of-war
Jelly slide
Flying bucket
Whirling wind speed meter
Ping pong flinger
Gas-fuelled rocket
Magnet power

Make it Bang!
978 0 7502 7731 0

See a bang
Bang, twang, pop!
How a bang travels
The speed of a bang
Bangs and whispers
The screaming cup
High and low
The sounds of speech
Solid sounds
Stop that banging!
Find the bang
How musical are you?

Make it Change!
978 0 7502 7734 1

Turn a penny green!
Lava volcano
The red cabbage test
Exploding drinks
Make salt disappear
 and reappear
Rubbery bones
Bottle balloon
Magic ice cubes
Plastic bag ice cream
Pure water still
Make your own butter
Mould garden

Make it Grow!
978 0 7502 7736 5

Egg-head!
What makes plants grow?
Supermarket sprout!
Black bag balloon
Make a thermometer
Expanding ice
Sugary strings
Grow your own stalactites
Microwave a marshmallow
Popcorn!
Make bread rise
Squirty cream challenge

Make it Glow!
978 0 7502 7733 4

Light and shadows
Periscope
Tea light lanterns
Make an indoor rainbow
Glowing envelopes, plasters
 and sweets!
Glow-in-the-dark shapes
Make a glowing jar lantern
Glow stick photos
Glowing water stream
Laser jelly
Camera obscura
Ultraviolet glow

Make it Splash!
978 0 7502 7735 8

Make a splash
Does water have a skin?
Upside-down cup
Water balloon pop!
Why do boats float?
Rising raisins
Magic liquid levels
Melted crayon art
The saliva test
Make your own river
Strange gloop
More water fun